The Ethereal Poetry Of Words
By Rachel Lawson

The Ethereal Poetry Of Words

Poetry

Rachel Lawson

Published by Rachel Lawson, 2023.

Table of Contents

The Ravens

A flock of ravens floats upon the air over their prey,
Like a looming black storm cloud of gloom,
In the later hours of the death of the day,
They fight each other for room,
In the melee, one is injured it falls,
Blood and gore fill the air,
The air is filled with their dire calls,
Little did the observers of this carnage care,
To them, it was merely a display of the nature of the raven,
Upon the hour they fled,
They were neither crazed nor craven,
They were happy and well-fed.

Flesh and Bone

I am but flesh and bone,
as such I have a lot to atone,
I consume the grasses of life,
to feed my flesh which is the living's fief,
my blood runs with the grass's essence,
my life requires its obsolescence,
the blood and flesh life's frame,
I am but bones in death as the Earth life's frame does reclaim,
life's form melts back to the Earth its mother,
the dirt of the body brings life to another,
the flesh in death feeds the grasses above,
life feeds upon the grass to feed their flesh and the cycle continues
thereof.

Death's Token

Upon my grave do not grieve,
Just leave upon it death's token in reprieve,
A single lily fear not my grave be not chilly,
It is the home of love I am now in heaven far above.

Lost in the sea of time

I am lost in the sea of time,
drowning in its waters,
falling in its depths,
the past present and future are one,
good-bye all hope and wonder,
I am lost for all time,
within the sea of time.

What's Left Unsaid

The biggest regret is not unfinshed thoughts,
It is what is unsaid the goodbyes, the I love yous and the like,
the things undone, the last thoughts of people would
seldom be on thoughts unthought because they rarely come to mind,
at least as import actions or lack of actions cause more pain.

We are just stardust

the stars are our mothers and fathers,
the elements of our bodies come from them,
as is too with the soul, the mind, the I am,
we but living stardust,
thinking star children looking for more,
we think we must,
are we alone or do we have family in space,
we forget we are one race,
the children of the stars,
the brothers and sisters of Earth and Mars

The Coming of the Storm

Lightening flashed and thunder boomed,
grey storm clouds loomed,
the air electric,
the air smelt of rain dirty and metallic
lightening strikes a tree it smoulders and burns,
the rain started slowly then hissed and the fire fizzed as the storm
churns
the rain washed lightly at the fire but the fire did not cease the tree was
doomed
Lightening flashed and thunder boomed.

Seven Pillars of Wisdom

"The Lord is my light." he guided me all my life,
he guided me from birth and through my strife,
a Prince of men known and admired by all who I call a friend,
I travelled to Arabia where which I alone defend,
I helped free Damascus from the Ottoman Turk,
although some say I went berserk,
a free Arabia was always my dream,
after the war, I was accused of going Arab or to them it did seem,
I returned to real life and tried to hide,
my legend had grown too much for me to abide,
I could not be me!
Although the world could not see,
one day I rode hell for leather on my motorcycle near Clouds Hill my
home,
I had a serious accident no longer did I roam,
I died and upon my grave, they wrote "Dominus illuminatio mea,"
"The Lord is my light." by those words my life did adhere.

Lost In The Shadows Of The Past

I am lost and forgotten as a living being,
Lost in the grim dark shadows of death,
I live in legend and as a vague memory of life,
I am as I was but am nothing but dust and bone,
A mere curiosity of a life lived, a requiem.
Lost in the shadows of the past, forgotten to time

Nevermore

Nevermore shall I see your face in this world,
I am lost and alone,
I miss your smile,
You are lost to the world,
Sleeping in the eternal sleep of death,
In your cold grave,
I kneel by your grave,
I feel nearer to you,
Even though we are far from each other,
Between us are life and death,
The furthest distance in space and time,
I reach in my dreams to see you,
To hear your voice again,
I reach out to you in my dreams,
Only to have you disappear like a wisp,
In the wind,
You disappear,
To return to me Nevermore

Gone with the Summer

You left me with the summer,
why did you have to go-
and not take me with you,
I miss you more than life,
I miss you in your death,
you were my life now-
I feel dead in this world-
without your voice and your touch,
I am all alone I need you so much,
all I can do is cry on your grave,
the Autumn leaves blow past-
us and I feel I'm with you again-
only for a moment, I close my eyes and
dream of you as the wind blows my hair,
I remember your touch,
I dream of the summer when you were with me,
I took you and life for granted,
I thought you and I were eternal,
but the autumn winds blew us apart,
all I have is now a rose on a grave between us,
I am lost and alone crying in the rain.

Sky Diamonds

Diamonds made of air,
Too precious to share,
Diamonds made by man,
Made only as scientists and dreamers can.

Softly Falls The Rain

Softly falls the rain, through the air cool, clear and crisp,
from the skies above, slowly falling to the ground,
falls the nectar of the sky, the balm of the Earth,
that moisturises soil, and nourishes the plants,
it the fills the oceans with it's waters, for the fish in it to swim,
and upon it men to sail, to catch the fish and
after the water brings life to the world. it returns to it's sky home and
waits to fall again.

The Reign of Rain

Cool and softly falls the rain,
from the silvery sky,
it comes sweetly hissing on my roof,
refreshing the world with its life-giving nectar.

The Silver Realm

The fading ghost of daylight melts into night,
The silver light of night starts it's haunting,
The light of the eventide melts in to the crystalline waters silver,
The ghostly light of night takes over the world,
It bewitches the heart and soul

Dreams

Words are the dreams the heart makes,
They are the wishes of the mind,
They are the heartaches and sighs,
They are the breaths and cries,
They are the life and end,
The light and dark,
They are the beauty of the night,
The warmth of the day,
The visions of the heart made real.

The Shadow of the Wind

Under the moon's silver glow
I heard the wind blow
the autumn leaves flew past me,
like charms in night's debris,
the wind it cools,
the night was full of the airs of scented jewels,
the breeze blew on the lake causing ripples of light and shadow,
I hear the wind's cries and see its tears which fly and show,
as crystalline glowing rain, it is the coming of a storm,
the shadows of the wind do form,
where the shadow of the wind does go
the aura of night shows in its glow.

The Marvellous Light

Crystalline pure silvery aura of night,
is within my sight,
the moon glows full and bright,
it is a marvellous light.

The Night Is Like A Beautiful Gem

The stars are silver sparkling gems floating in the onyx sea of pitch,
the moon like an illuminated glowing gem moonstone that swims
through the starlit sky,
the air is cool and misty upon the lake tonight,
the ground sparkles with its frosty carpet,
the night is like a beautiful gem tonight.

Yellow

I dream a dream so clear and mellow,
a soft sun glowing bright and yellow.
illuminating dawn dark and new,
the golden sun peeking out beneath the blue,
thick as golden honey

The Tapestries Above

I look in the night sky and see a black velvet band sown with diamonds that sparkle, and a giant round gem of moonstone closer in. The moonstone appears to sail through the velvet and diamonds of night's tapestry 'til dawn comes, with the raising of the golden tourmaline which is the day's star the sun which sails through the crystalline aquamarine skies of day tainted only with white, grey and pink wisps of magical shifting sand 'til eventide does come and night's tapestry returns.

Let it snow

Softly falls the snow,
making hearts aglow,
cool crisp,
floating in a wisp.

Reflections of Night

Sparkling jewels upon the water,
Come to my feverish mind,
Ethereal and enchanting like a lovers song,
Heady yet delicate like a mist at sea,
Glowing like my arduous heart,
A sight never to be forgot,
Lighting the night with their faint iridescence,
Dying with the dawn's light.

The Sparkling Skies Above

The stars are beautiful sparkling diamonds up on a dark velvet sky, they twinkle in constant rhythm in the cool refreshing night's air enchanting the heart and the soul down to the core.

The Gossamer Weave of Night

The starry night sky is gossamer only visible beneath the moonlight's
glow like the web of a spider,
it enchants the eye and the mind in it's dreamy twinkle like sparkling
diamonds on a black velvet sky,
the moon is like the gem moonstone glowing in it's lonely vigil,
the darkness is cut by the light of the moon's glow.

The Sparkling Roof Tops of the World

They say the night has a thousand eyes,
That "One could not count the moons that shimmer on her roofs, or the
thousand splendid suns that hide behind her wall."
Beautiful sparkling eyes of stars the lonely travellers of the skies,
thy light charms all,
thy fires eternally burn,
the silvery beams from moons and suns illuminate the night with night's
alluring glow
the light of these hundred million suns and moons illuminate lovers
perpetual yearn,
they are distant and far memories of days aeons ago.

Catching Stars

The night is lonely and cold,
I wanted to do this before I get old,
I am a star hunter that's what I do,
I hunt for stars until the night is through,
with my net of night,
I catch their light,
I put it in jars like fireflies,
for me to go back on the hunt the night cries.

A Moon Shadow Nocturne

A play of light and dark,
under the wan light of the moon plays with the skipping shadows of
night's dance their bewitching saraband with the moonlight,
silver moonlight and darkness melt into one in the cool airs of the
nocturnal bower of night,
the stars sparkle in the shadows far above the worldly cradle of man,
it is pure enchantment by moonlight,
a nocturne of moonlight and shadows melding it to one,
a song both dark and light with an ethereal heady air of enchantment
leaving the heart aglow

Nocturne or the music of the night : Extended

The night is like music it is cool and crisp,
smooth and elegant,
the stars twinkle like music,
the moon sails across the sky like a music score,
the darkness is the beat of the heart listening to music or looking in the
mystery which is the night,
the night enthrals like a sweet riff of music,
the beauty of the night is the music of the stars,
the ghostly light of night is like an aria soft,
a song of the night is the unearthly glow,
the ethereal atmosphere of the night is like a favourite song,
night tugs on the heartstrings like a beautiful voice in song,
it is the music of the night

Moonlight

Under the crystalline wan pale silver light of the moon,
I bath in the ethereal glow of the night,
I watch the play of light and dark in the sky,
the stars sparkle in the black velvet sky,
the mystic moon shines magically above, illuminating the world below
with her enchanting shimmering, glimmering, glow

Moonlight Nocturne

Under the ardent Moon's glow
I watch her traverse the night
in her heavenly bower above
illuminating the world below
with her bright radiant aura
in her silvery realm of night
stealing the hearts and minds
of those beneath her with her
enchanting light that illuminates
the night with her sisters the stars

A Starlight Nocturne

In the liquid crystalline silver starlight
I bath in the light of a full silver Moon,
watching the night sky enchanted by
its beauty is serene and calming it is,
the air is cool and fresh on my skin and
my lungs, it refreshes with it's chill,
the air is filled with the scent of night jasmine,
the songs of frogs on the water and crickets
envelopes the area with their ethereal music

The Moonless Night

the moon is hiding,
the stars are shining,
the night is crisp,
the clouds are a wisp,
the night is dark,
the light is stark,
I look at the stars,
I wonder can I see Mars,
I know not the sky,
still I watch the stars go by,
I like a moonless night,
the stars are quite a sight.

Moonlight on the Water

A sparkling river cool and clear,
enchanted by nature's beauty divine,
pure elegance to the eye and mind.

The Mystery of Night

They say the night has a thousand Eyes,
It's beauty no one denies,
The nocturnal passing is cool and crisp,
The mind creates ghosts from a single wisp,
No man knows night truly,
Man knows it comes by dark and cooly,
It has a feeling of enchantment,
Beholders are usually lost in the moment,
The glazed eye that is the moon comes ever slowly,
In the dark speckled sky, people watch them longingly,
As they float by in night's procession,
They travel by with great precision,
Til the dawn time chorus comes,
And the day It becomes.

The Dark Mystery of Night

It is a play of light and dark,
illuminated by a silvery spark,
what lies hidden out of sight,
it is the dark mystery which is the night.

Moon Rise

The moon rises from a dark burning sea,
ink black clouds like smoke float between it and me,
the land is as dark as the night sky,
the clouds like smoke over the fiery water float by.

Night

Dark and cool,
clear and crisp,
your heart is hard to see,
your silver aura the heart inspires,
beauty is in the observer's eye,
you bear an air of enchantment,
Night comes to bewitch the soul,
the sparkling stars are like a glass of good champagne,
pure and clear is thy nocturnal glow,
like a ballad thy beauty,
the moon is exquisite in its charm and light,
the night is the jewel of the day.

The air is of silver and pearl, the night is liquid with moonlight- extended

The stars are silver diamonds placed upon a black velvet sky,
the leaves in the wind are gems floating in the cool crisp air,
the rain is falling stars like glowing diamonds,
the river is crystalline rippling mercury beneath the full moon's light,
the night is full of the sounds of life,
crickets chirp, frogs croak, night birds sing their sweet serenade of night,
my boat cuts through the river with a soft swish of water,
an ethereal glowing fog is hiding the river in patches,
the air is full of the scents of flowers on the shore,
the moon is like the gem moonstone bright and clear peaking out of the
clouds are shadowy faintly glowing cotton candy mist,
"The air is of silver and pearl, the night is liquid with moonlight."
I am breathless.

The Edge of Night

In the beginning, there was night,
then cutting through the darkness came a light,
and from it burst time,
from the primordial soup grew matter ringing like a chime,
then aeons later sprung life from light and matter,
matter and life, time did batter,
life, matter a light all in time end,
leaving nothing but night to ascend.

Some Truths Live Beyond Other Truths, Whoever Said Those Truths Have To Be Actually True

Not all truths are actually true, sometimes the stories we tell ourselves
and our dreams the hidden truths live beyond the time the facts are long
dead and forgotten.
Anyone can quote Shakespeare, but the man himself and his life lies lost
in the shadows of the past.

The Tempest's End

The air is crisp and clean it smells dirty and metallic,
the rain has died to a fine mist that hugs the ground,
the wet pavement has a feel of the ethereal and mystic,
this aura is only seen after a summer storm is around.

Liquid Gold

smoother than honey,
like a golden sunset sunny,
rich as glowing golden honey,
thick and runny,
worth more than money.

Stardust: extended

The universe is made of stardust,
we are all made of stardust,
all that ever lived and all that are to come,
are just variations of stardust,
we come from stardust and to stardust, we end

A cool refreshing dip in a limpet pool azure

I slowly wade through an azure limpet pool,
I look for crabs and such in this pool the water cool,
the sun beats down and warms me and makes pretty azure shadows
below on the sands,
I run my fingers through the water it is refreshingly cooling on my
hands,
I know I must go I love this memory so I cry,
then I hang my thoughts out to dry.

The Stars Shine Down

The stars shine down from the black velvet sky
the shining smiling Moon rolls by way up high,
the Earth below is, illuminated by their light,
they are the eternal sentinels of the night.

Forever Autumn

I am trapped in a world of Autumn,
the season of the fall,
leaves of rainbow colours do fall,
skies of deepest blue,
strong winds blow the leaves in the trees,
the leaves float through the sky like feathers in the wind,
the leaves fall in deep rainbow coloured carpets.
its beauty will remain forever in my mind.

Requiem

Under the moon's silver glow,
I could forget everything and live in this moment forever,
it tugs on the heartstrings like a beautiful voice in song,
words are the dreams the heart makes,
all now of the dream I have is a requiem.

The Power of Words

The crystalline essence of words is rich and syrupy,
clear and crisp,
strong and smooth,
dare you find the light in the darkness,
that illuminates the night with words purity and glow.

The Ocean

The water gently laps upon the shore
with a cheery swish of water hitting the sand,
it bears a magical air of relaxation,
to the listener's ear, mind, and soul.

The Destruction of Time

Nothingness starts with a single chip,
a sea over time can wash away a stone,
a bird can chip away a tree with time,
mountains melt in rivers and seas,
time erodes all to nonexistence

Dreaming

A fantasy world is dreaming,
beyond wakeful deeming,
nothing is as it should be,
nothing is beyond what you can see,
floating through the air,
without a worry or care,
that is all in a dream,
nothing is what it may seem.

Time Travel

I am a time traveler, as are we all, we travel through time moment by moment, the possibility of time and chance are considered possible in parallel universes, we all live on in this universal life, balancing upon the tightrope which is time and choice, controlling in which parallel world within which we live and die.

The Rose of Snow

Once existed a pure white rose,
from the snow, it rose,
a rose of purest snow,
from the snow, it did grow,
and by the snow, it did die,
in death, it was petals in the snow it did lie.

Saturn

Rings and diamonds,
a precious gem of space,
planet of ice and rock,
pressure under beauty,
diamonds melting into crystalline liquid diamonds in death.

Like a Moth to a Flame

Humans chase the sun like a moth to a flame,
we rise with the sun and hibernate when the sun leaves,
We adore her sister the moon who is lit by the sun's loving glow,
The sun warms our hearts in our Earthly bower.

Stars of fire, Stars of ice

they eternally burn with their hearts of fire,
their deaths can be dire,
some shrink die dark and colder than ice,
others die with a bang and implode the scientists hypothesise,
It's a toss of a dice
for the stars of fire and a stars of ice.

Requiem for a Dream

I grieve the loss of a dream,
I feel like from me tore a seam,
I lost my faith and hope with it,
I am lost sad and lonely I admit,
I fear life without the dream I bore,
I was happy in the light of my dream before,
I feel my dream has died,
I feel it to me had lied.
will you my dream just fade away,
disappear in an echo of pain one day as dreams do decay.

The River of Light- the true music of the night

I hear a river washing upon the shores,
I see a river of light washing through the night's shore,
They wash is softly in the night which seems their home,
The night is dark and starlight is seen from my window,
The moon, a plate of shining silver snow hanging in the sky like a
diamond bright,
The crystalline river is the light of many a car on the road driving in a
line,
The wave's sound is the sound of car engines revving,
It is a modern river of night.

The End

Rachel is a prolific author and a lover of Gothic poetry and the stories of Emily Dickinsen, Poe, and other poets and writers. she writes in a Gothic sometimes romantic, and somewhat eclectic style. Rachel is a distant relative and big fan of the famous but little know writer Fanny Burney.

Don't miss out!

Visit the website below and you can sign up to receive emails whenever Rachel Lawson publishes a new book. There's no charge and no obligation.

https://books2read.com/r/B-A-HMGO-CKKSC

BOOKS 2 READ

Connecting independent readers to independent writers.

Did you love *The Ethereal Poetry Of Words*? Then you should read *The Magicians Mega Omnibus*[1] by Rachel Lawson!

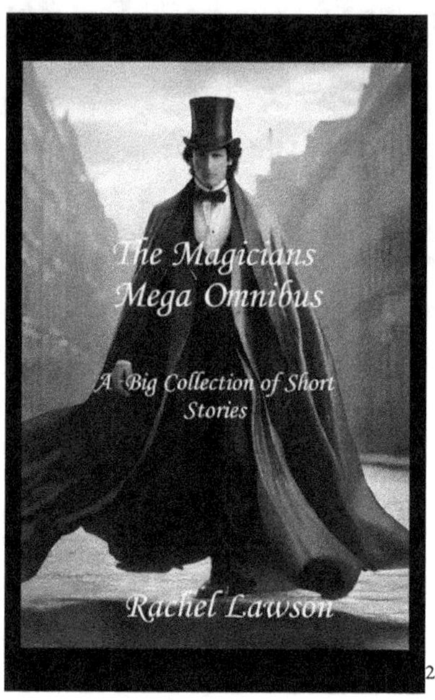

A feast of short stories from Rachel Lawson's The Magicians series. Note this is the text version and this book is also available a audio book.

Starting with * Star Crossed

A Novelette

The Necromantor, the King of Doom meets his match with a grey alien diplomat's sister Mookaite Ga her brother tries to break them up not because of racism but because he's a jinx because all women he loves die according to the drunk Masked Chicken. They have Romeo and Juliet relationship. It all goes wrong when the press turns up and the secret lovers are caught revealing the existence of aliens and their relationship. Will it help or hinder their relationship?

---

1. https://books2read.com/u/mvBoYX

2. https://books2read.com/u/mvBoYX

The book ends with The Requiem a short story where the ghost of one the Magicians goes to his own funeral drunk.

Most of the stories have a gothic dark fantasy or horror feel. The order of the book here:

Starcrossed

The Cult of Death

The Innocent Killer

The Grudge

The Last Dance

Left for dead

Danse Macabre

Fetch

Alien invasion

Surrender offers rest, But I'd die for peace

Broken

Hell is Empty and All the Devils Are Here

The Necromancer goes to jail

Jasper's Fate

The Emperor is dead, long live the King

The requiem

Read more at https://rachellawsonpoet.yolasite.com/.

Also by Rachel Lawson

Poetry
Night Poetry
Requiem for a Dream
A Moon Shadow Nocturne
The Pearl of Night
The Song of My Pen
Tempus Fugit Time Flies: Time pieces
The Ethereal Poetry Of Words

Stand Alone
The White Knight

Stand and Deliver
In The Moonlight
The King's Man
In The Moonlight & Shadows in the Daylight
Shadows in the Daylight
The King's Man
Shadows in the Moonlight
Stand and Deliver

The King's Man

The Magicians
Getting Good Ratings Is Murder
Blind Faith
Once In a Blue Midnight
The Manchurian Candidate
The Gift And Other Short Stories
Vivienne and the Reaper The Mortal Coil Extended
The Grinch Returns
Danse Macabre
Hello From The Dark-Side
Hit The Road Jack
* Star Crossed
The scariest monsters are the ones that lurk within our souls
The Rose
The Masked Magician
Hello Darkness, My Old Friend
* Star Crossed
* Star Crossed
Shadow Play
Hit The Road Jack
The Magicians Mega Omnibus
Times Change
Danse Macabre And Other Stories
Legends Of Yore
The Haunting Of The Necromancer And Other Stories
The Mask Magician and other stories
The Man Who Sold The World
The King of Doom
Christmas is Hell

Everyone Is An Alien Somewhere
The Long Dark Night of the Soul
The Necromancer goes to Jail
The Necromancer Goes To Jail
The Innocent Killer
The Dark Side
Coming of the Angel of Death
The Picture of Death and Other Stories
A Very Grim Christmas And Other Stories
* Star Crossed - Reworked
The Locket And The Thief And Other Stories
Tales Of The Necromancer
Once In A Blue Midnight

Standalone
What The-?

Watch for more at https://rachellawsonpoet.yolasite.com/.